The Digital Age

A Critical View from a Wisdom Perspective

by OM C. Parkin

Gateways Books and Tapes

Nevada City, California

2018

ISBN: 978-0-89556-287-6
First Gateways Books edition
Text © 2018 by OM C. Parkin
All Rights Reserved

Original Edition from Advaita Media, Germany:
Das digitale Zeitalter aus Sicht der Weisheitslehre
Translated from the German original by Matthias Schossig
Edited by Anama Frühling

ISBNs:
978-0-89556-287-6 paperback
978-0-89556-631-7   pdf
978-0-89556-633-1 kindle / mobi-pocket
978-0-89556-634-8 EPUB

Cover & Graphic Design by Gailyn Porter, based on the German
edition

Published by: Gateways Books and Tapes
IDHHB, Inc.
PO Box 370
Nevada City, CA 95959
USA
Phone: (800) 869-0658 or (530) 271-2239
E-mail: info@gatewaysbooksandtapes.com
Website: http://www.gatewaysbooksandtapes.com

Author's Foreword

"What we are currently experiencing is much more than an industrial revolution. It is something that will transcend not only human beings, but life itself." A new, artificial life would emerge, "a life that is more robust and spreads beyond our biosphere, colonizing and making the Milky Way and eventually the entire universe intelligent." These words come from Jürgen Schmidhuber, the scientific director of the Research Institute for Artificial Intelligence IDSIA near Lugano (Switzerland) and they convey the full extent of the euphoria of so-called transhumanists in the face of the revolution of the digital age, which will finally provide the technical means to liberate people from their shabby, decayed condition, the *conditio humana*. The I always knew that it deserves something else than this limited condition, and so it thinks its big chance has finally come: The completion of its project immortality. In the view of the starry-eyed rationalist who begins to study the writings of Perennial Philosophy, there is indeed a great deal of agreement here. After all, have the great wisdom teachings of humanity from East and West, at their core, not always pursued only one goal: To make the knowledge of eternal life accessible to the student on the path? Do digitalists who believe that true, unlimited life is found online, and transhumanists who believe in enlightenment by technical means, not pursue the same goal?

This little book describes a tragic misunderstanding and its consequences. This misunderstanding has its roots in the limited state of consciousness of the founding fathers of the digital revolution and it continues in many of its enthusiastic supporters. "They are all subject to a serious *internal/external level confusion.*" This book presents a dialogue with students (some working in the computer industry themselves or are professionally dealing with digital media), which emerges from this statement.

All of the highest inner teachings, as described by the perennial philosophy (Advaita, Zen, Christian mysticism, Sufism, etc.), actually point to an experiential path that results in the realization of the True Self and thus in immortality. However, this realization of immortality can only take place by virtue of mortality: "Die before you die," is an important instruction of inner teachings and their masters, pointing to the conscious dying of a mental entity called the I. This instruction can only be taken to heart by students on the inner path, because the inner path teaches them a distinction between I and Non-I, a distinction between mind and soul. It is the intelligence of this intrinsic discernment that can prevent the momentous confusion that is expressed in so many deluded followers of the digital revolution: the confusion of true inner freedom and fear-driven megalomania.

The digital revolution itself is neither a curse nor a blessing to humanity. The difference is in our consciousness. People who are interested in true freedom follow the unwritten laws of the Dharma, the inner practice, as students of all generations have done. In that regard, the digital age is changing precisely— nothing.

OM C. PARKIN, Gut Saunstorf, September 2018

The Digital Age

A Critical View from a Wisdom Perspective

OM C. Parkin

OM C. Parkin

The Digital Age from the Viewpoint of the Wisdom Teachings

Question: *We are undergoing the so-called "Digital Revolution," which was triggered by the invention of the computer, and there is a term that is associated with this, namely the "Second Modernity." The "First Modernity" was about muscle power being replaced by steam engines, and now in the "Second Modernity," it is important that the brain power of the people is replaced by artificial intelligence.*
Where are we?

OM: I do not know. From the point of view of the eternal wisdom teachings, the "Digital Age" is not a revolution, it is not even a point of reference. The digital revolution will change the external world very much, in a good way, but also in a bad way, that is for sure. And it also marks a step in human evolution. But the eternal wisdom teachings and their laws will remain entirely unimpressed. This revolution is led by idealistic self-proclaimed benefactors of humanity from the Silicon Valley in California, who share a big misunderstanding. They are all subject to a serious *internal/external levels confusion.*

This is a rather unwieldy term that you have used frequently. Does it mean that they become unable to distinguish between the internal and the external world?

In the minds of these digital conquistadores, there is the belief in a doctrine of salvation for the whole human race through technological progress, which is supposed to substitute for religion. In other words: They confuse the seemingly infinite creative possibilities of the digital revolution and the life-enhancing conditions for many people in the world that they may be able to create with an awakening path for humanity. An awakening path is an inner path, and the leading heads of this revolution will probably not even know what an inner path is. Do you know why I find Apple© so unsympathetic?

Why do you find Apple so unsympathetic?

Not that their products are bad. On the contrary. It is the spirit. Apple is a good example for what I called "the descent of the sacred into the dullness of the material world" in the book *Intelligence of Awakening*[1]. They consciously drive a mystification, a quasi-religious excitement about a product that ultimately nobody needs. A good example was their advertising for their iPhone: "If you don't have an iPhone, well, you don't have an iPhone." This is pure megalomania. Following that, an artist arranged an installation at the Altona train station in Hamburg, with a giant iPhone showing a different advertising message: "If you don't have a soul, at least you have an iPhone." From the viewpoint of *reality*[2] it is completely immaterial whether there is an iPhone, or not. I could not care less about it. It is a testimony to the poverty of the soul and extreme naivety, when people, who are eager to purchase the next device, spend the entire night in front of the Apple Store, just to be the first ones who are able to walk out of the store with the device in their hands. The consequence of this mystification is that many owners of an Apple product, who suffer from a lack of self-worth, believe they hold a precious totem in their hands, which is charged with a force that is able to increase the value and meaning of their ego-mind.

This descent of the sacred, commercially exploited by many companies (all of them manufacturing something that ultimately nobody needs) is a purely blasphemous act, initiated by people who in their own spiritual world suffer this descent of the sacred into a world which is more or less devoid of significance and depth itself. This descent inevitably leads to a confusion of the internal with the external.

The replacement of the thinking capacity by artificial intelligence in the "second modernity," as you suggest in your question, has quite a lot of advantages. It means, for example, that we no longer need to save each and every known fact in our minds (a brain researcher would say "in our brains.") A few mouse clicks are sufficient to reel it in from the Internet. Artificial intelligence can be seen as the exposure of the thinking mind as a machine with inadequate properties. We could therefore focus on essential knowledge, which is never to be found on the Internet: The knowledge of the *Self.*

You also called the digital age a sublimation of the technocratic age. Does this, from the point of view of the wisdom teachings, imply also a collective developmental step, an evolutionary ascent?

3

The introduction of the digital age has the potential to be the external reflection of a collective overcoming of the limitations of a purely rational intelligence. The limits of linear thinking will be blown out of the water and the next stage in the development of consciousness, the *integral aperspective level* is approaching. This term was coined by the consciousness researcher Jean Gebser[3]. In his main work *The Ever-Present Origin* (first part), he writes about this level of awareness: "We understand this as ... the completion of wholeness, i.e. the recovery of an intact, original state in an enriching inclusion of all previous performance. ... The restoration of the 'dimension' of the human." What Gebser describes here is the integration of the Spirit in the human artifact. So how can the digital revolution contribute to leaving behind the developmental stage of a purely rational intelligence?

The digital age is also the age of information, since one of its characteristics is the increasingly complex networking, the provision and dissemination of information. Information is the content of the mental world. This means that the essence of the digital age is of a mental nature. In the inner order of the theory of evolution of human consciousness, this constitutes the final ascent to the third brain and the potential advancement of human consciousness into the realm of the subtle.

Sublimation is the evolutionary advancement in the direction of a *spiritualization of* the human being liberated from the entanglements of the gross material world. *Spiritualization*[4] is therefore the expansion and increasing subtleness of human consciousness, a goal of the realization of the human evolution, taught by mystics of all times. However, this should be described in a subjunctive clause, because for the general population the digital revolution shows no signs of a *spiritualization* at all. This can only take place on an inner path. The digital revolution is more of a *mentalization*.

Mentalization is the rotten fruit of an unhinged, disintegrated developmental path of a person lost in the labyrinth of a virtual mental world, because all the stages of development, which are the foundation of a culminating *spiritualization*, are truncated, or only partially accessible. In any case, they are not integrated in a healthy way. *Mentalization* is also a description of the state in which the main faculty of discernment on the inner path is lost; the *real* can no longer be discerned from *the unreal*. The *mentalization* itself is an artificial, non-real state, which is only imitating true *spiritualization*. The digital revolution, which will not be satisfied with artificial intelligence alone, but is obsessed with the creation of artificial *consciousness*, is doomed to exponentially escalate the collective *mentalization*. Certain parts of the nerd culture already show the tendency to become the archetype of the detached mental being, disembodied, emotionally crippled, socially challenged to a pathological degree, anemic. A type that is as virtual as the world in which he is lost.

Are you saying that the digital revolution is actually the sign of an ascent of human consciousness, in which the physical level for the purpose of self-preservation is becoming less and less important, also in working life? Is the nerd just an extreme, or is it a figure, an archetype as you say, who, in an extreme form, shows what also applies for the general population?

The nerd will no longer be the exception but is becoming more and more the rule. An addictive personality under the spell of the virtual world, completely lacking any rootedness in his heart center. A healthy and harmonious growth of human consciousness demands an *integral way.* Integral evolution is not a linear ascent, as the ladder model suggests[5], but an ascent which allows for a counterbalancing descent, also described as the *involutive arc*[6]. *Evolution* needs *involution* in order to be integral. The *spiritualization* of the human as the fruit of an evolutionary advancement can only mature if the ascent is rooted in a descent. The higher needs to be rooted in the lower. Wings need roots. The expansive forces of the *evolutionary arc* need to balance the reductive forces of the *involutive arc.*

You can substantiate this anchoring? In your textbook on the inner path, The Intelligence of Awakening, you use the metaphysical concept of the "three brains of the human being," which divides the evolution of human consciousness roughly into three stages, in accordance with the "law of the three." I assume that by "anchoring" you mean the evolutionary anchoring in the lower levels of development, the lower brains?
The *three brains* are a description of a simplified sequence of stages of development of the human person. The *first*

brain, the gut center, is the physical anchoring. This is also the anchoring in the realm of sensory perception. The *second brain*, the heart center, is the anchoring in the feeling nature of man, and the *third brain* is the anchoring in the spiritual world. Few people continue to develop into the transcendent, transpersonal condition of the *fourth brain*[7]. Any form of a higher, evolutionary level of human consciousness holds within itself the potential for *dissociations*, so that the lower level is not completely and soundly integrated with the next higher level.

In the first millennium, something extraordinary happened in the evolution of human consciousness, a process which can be seen as the original sin. An unprecedented spirit began to emerge from its unconscious origins and—for the first time ever—consciously said: "I." The *thinking mind* stepped into the light of the world and henceforth called it "My World."

This means that before the first millennium B.C. there was no thinking mind in man?

No. What we today call the *thinking mind*, that mentally operating I from which we quite naturally seem to operate in our practice of the inner path, did not exist before. The same incarnation impulse, the same demasking, we can observe on the individual level in each small child. The mind reveals itself only after it is emerging from its physical, *tamas*-like fusion.[8]

But this was not the spiritualization of which you spoke? The spiritualization for the common people? The collective ascent?

No, to the contrary, because the mind separated from its roots, i.e. it lost its anchoring. It was an ascent, yes, and it was necessary but for the common people it was not an integrated ascent, and the painful consequences are lasting until today. In fact, we have not even reached the high point of the visible consequences.

In his book *The Next Development in Mankind,* L.L. Whyte, a Scottish scientist and evolution researcher (†1972), describes a *collective dissociation of the occident*, which began around 500 B.C. and continues to this day as "European dissociation," a dissociation of body and mind, a missing anchoring of the mind in the body. This is a collective mental disorder of the West, which I call the "regular madness" of Westerners because it is completely mainstream. "The mind (the thinking mind) constantly has difficulties with the simpler world of instinctive impulses and therefore tends to dissociate from nature (i. e. also from the body)," writes Ken Wilber.[9] Already, the collective "European dissociation" has lasted for over 2500 years. It is a serious matter and is critical for exploitative, disintegrated aberrations of society against nature, originating in the occident, first in the industrialization, and now in the digitization.

I will tell you about an experience to give you an example, what the lack of an anchoring in the lower brains can cause:

When I was in Mumbai, India, I made a day trip to a nearby island, Elephant Island, a very special place with over a thousand years old sacred temple sites. There are caves with sixteen foot tall Shiva statues of impressive grandeur. A place to receive with all the senses, with an open heart and a quiet mind, to breathe, to witness, to realize. A place to sit in silence and to meditate. But the Indian day tourists who populated this place, seemed not to be interested in the place. They were only interested in their mobile phones in order to send messages, to make calls, or to take photographs. Not even photos of these sacred monuments, but selfies— in the foreground: the center of the universe, myself; in the background: the sacred monuments as a backdrop for the I. It was an atmosphere of ignorance, which was hard to bear: disturbed people visiting sacred places to celebrate an ego of which nobody knows who that is. This experience left a strong impression, and it shows the disastrous consequences of a lack of anchoring, both in the present world of sensations, the physical presence of the moment *(first brain)*, as well as the feeling presence *(second brain)*. And it also demonstrates the very practical consequences of *mentalization,* life in a virtual world of digitization. The actual, integral experience in the reality of the moment is sacrificed in favor of *images of reality*. A clear indication of the total loss of essential discernment. Who does not remember the second commandment, "Thou shalt not make unto thee a graven image"? But the real significance of this commandment, its entire scope and its far-reaching consequences only a few have realized. By means of the new technologies of the digital world, the madness of the thinking mind, to capture everything in images, is being reinvigorated. (Images are nothing but pre-rational thought forms.) The flow of impermanence, in which nothing can be grasped, is lost, and this is precisely what this is all about. Behind these seemingly harmless phenomena of the surface and the ordinary, the ego schemes to accomplish its sole purpose: its immortality.

You are saying that the digital revolution cannot be classified as consciousness development, nor as a false consciousness development. It can be both. Does this also apply for the counter-movement? I am thinking of impulses like "Back to Nature," "Back to community," "Slowing down," etc. Do you see that there are some healthy processes of an involutive arc? Or would you see that as a regression as well?

In regards to the counter-movement, we must make the distinction as well. Therefore I make the distinction between a conscious and unconscious arc in the downward spiral of the *involutive arc* in exactly the same way as in the upward spiral of the *evolutionary arc*. What we commonly understand under *regression* is a quasi-synonym for the unconscious involutive arc, which cannot be a cure for an unconscious evolutionary arc. We do not need to go "back to nature," as for example the Amish people understand that by only using horse-drawn carriages for transportation because they reject technological progress. Similarly, there is no need for us to eat like the *noble wild* of the Stone Age as the paleo diet gurus proclaim. That is regression. An integral evolution, which is a true progress, requires an integration of nature. That is precisely what is wrong with the collective dissociation of the occident (*European dissociation*) mentioned above, which is a misguided development with disastrous consequences for the planet; keywords: climate change, extinction of species, pollution of the oceans, exploitation of the rain forest and, and, and.

As a remedy for this dissociation you describe the concept of 'conscious regression.'

First and foremost, this is the reconnection to the heart center (*second brain*). The opening of the heart center is of great importance for Western people. If a student is taught this reconnection on the path of experience no concept of "slowing down" is necessary. The deceleration is happening completely by itself, because the heart center has by nature a slower frequency than the mental center. The deeper we descend into the depth of our being, the slower the inner frequency becomes. This is why I feel a certain degree of resistance against the frequency of both, mechanization and digitalization of the world, which is way too fast.

Against the frequency?

Yes, against the frequency, because I see a fundamental *internal/external level confusion*. This results in a link between the highly accelerated growth and progress in the outer world and the slowdown of the growth and progress in the inner world. In other words: If people externalize their life force and intelligence, nothing is available for the inner path. The overly fast external growth is paid for by a slow-down of internal growth. The would-be world conquerors of Silicon Valley do not see this connection. They believe in a one-way growth ideology, pure expansion without limits, which makes no distinction between the inner and the outer—which ironically turns out to be their limitation. They are unable to make the distinction because they apparently lack the internal faculties.

When the attention is drawn away from the internal, then the result is that you spend much time in the external, and the external is developing strongly. Or is it the rapid development in the external, which causes that you are developing more slowly?

Both. You describe a vicious circle. Do you believe that people would produce the same amount of consumer goods, and that they would have the same external frequency of action and of motion if they were on an inner journey? The increasingly accelerated development of the outer world as it happens through the mechanization and digitization, is driven by a mental investment, a mental engagement. This happens through a male mind, which transforms inner power into outer production, while disconnecting from the internal. First we described the loss of internal anchoring in the lower brains, but there is a more fundamental loss of anchoring of the ego (the development level of the mental I since the beginning of the "European dissociation"): The loss of inwardness. In order to understand the structures of this mental I (which I mostly call *thinking mind* or sometimes *ego*) the *enneagram of ego-structures*[10] is helpful. It shows that this *ego* is formed by complete externalization (enneatype 9, the archetype of the ego) during a process, which I also call the *outpouring of the soul*. The passion assigned to this ego-type is *indolence*, in form of a *psycho-spiritual inertia* that destroys every serious interest in the true self, in *reality*. The main consequence of this indolence is the loss of inwardness.

So who would have thought that a crucial mental-emotional driving factor for a too high frequency of the external development is *indolence*? *Indolence* leads to a significant decrease in the internal development frequency, to an inner slowdown.

If many more people would embark on an inner path, the frequency of the output power, the hectic over-productivity in the external (supposedly always in the service of prosperity) would decrease. Through the relocation of attention back to the internal from the external, the productivity in the external is slowing down in a natural way, because the "over-" falls away. A part of the life force is directed back to the development and productivity of internal processes, in order to liberate the pure consciousness, which is not ego-driven.

The wisdom teachings have no interest in the surface frequencies of the digital age. A computer that is outdated in three years is just a joke from the point of view of frequencies, in which the wisdom teachings operate. The awakening teaching that was already accessible 2000 years ago and is still accessible has remained the same and it will continue to do so. The mind of the masses changes, but not the teaching. Who is interested in finding the wisdom and reality of perennial philosophy will have to refrain from the fast and hectic frequencies of the surface of existence and venture into the deeper spheres in order to resonate there with very much slower frequencies. The deeper I fall into the layers of being, the slower the frequencies. Let us compare it with the ocean: On the surface, the waves appear with high frequency, every gust of wind has an immediate effect on the movement of the surface, while the currents of the deep sea move with a very much slower and quieter frequency. And on the bottom of the sea, it is very quiet.

If indolence slows down the internal development while contributing to the acceleration of the external development, does that mean that the people of our time tend to be too slow, internally?

No, quite the contrary. They are too fast for recognition; this means that the stupidity of worshiping the digital world has nothing to do with desensitization, with inner slowdown, with a lack of capacity. It has everything to do with the fact that the inner frequency is too high, too heady. Specifically, the thinking mind is much too fast and therefore the entire integral development of the human being is too slow. The mental center (the third brain) operates at high frequency, hyperactively, but it is not, or not sufficiently, connected with the heart center (the second brain). Internally, the descending arc is so severely weakened that the overall system has a weakened cognitive ability. Because the cognitive ability, which exceeds the rational, is not based on the thinking mind, but on the integration of the *three brains*—the *Great Flow*. When the Great Flow flows through us, it drives *integral intelligence*, which enables trans-rational knowledge. The discovery of the *Great Flow* in us requires *conscious regression,* the conscious inner re-descent, which releases *fixations*[11] in the lower brains and thus integrates the power into the flow of the *Great Cycle*. The reunification of the three brains is one of the goals of the inner path.

The nerd is also an excellent figure to illustrate the limited cognition.

He has certainly excellent combinatorial capabilities for networking in the virtual world which, however, are quite useless when it comes to the knowledge of the *Self*. Not even the smaller task of becoming an adult human being can be solved in the virtual world.

For the recognition of the reality in an integral way, a holistic way, the way of the *three brains*, is needed, which—through their opening—create together an integral frequency of the whole organism, a heart frequency. The heart frequency of this organism is the median frequency, mediating between the high spiritual and the lower, long wave, physical frequencies.

I think you are designing a pretty gloomy scenario. Namely that the "digitization" and the "Information Age" with their speed help to create an ever faster external frequency, to create something which may be able to fill the big holes in the internal life. The digitization therefore is perfectly suited to escalate the vicious circle of increasing inner emptiness and increasing compensatory external productivity.

This is true.

Wouldn't then a "Burnout" be the natural consequence of this alienation?

I am neither optimistic nor pessimistic. I just demonstrate potential tendencies. No one can precisely predict the development. I merely describe the "Information Age" from the point of view of the wisdom teachings, which gives a different interpretation of the flood of information suddenly available. These teachings lead me into an inner depth, in which only the essential is of concern. From this perspective, a large part of the Internet, the information disseminated in social networks, is nothing but mental waste. Produced by an endless self-entertainment machinery of the ego. It is mental pollution. The information age is also the age of a mental pollution of the atmosphere.

Any journalist would immediately think of "fake news" or "post-factual" ideas.

This is just the smallest part. I am speaking of a much broader internal compensation through the process of *rationalization.*[12] The overproduction in the material world is increasingly shifting into the mental world. The thinking mind constantly wants to consume, first physical products, then information. We have arrived in the age of information gluttony. *Gluttony* is an old concept, quasi-synonymous with greed, which shows the madness: Filling oneself up as an end in itself. It is no longer about content, it is just about the filling. To escape from fear, because greed is just a derivative of fear. Even deeper: To escape from the inner emptiness. This triggers a process of inner erosion. In a text about the news hunger of the consumer it says: "We consume details about the world in order to hide from the world."[13] Not only from the world, would I like to add, but above all from ourselves.

But these trends will also cause counter-reactions on different levels. A new "Offline-App," in which the user can set different levels of accessibility on his smartphone, is addressing the symptoms rather than the cause. In 2015, a political scientist from Berlin published a book under the characteristic title: *Analog is the new Organic.* However, all these externalized discussions about the shadow of digitization are not questioning the naive world view, which assumes that the distinctions of *online* and *offline* or *digital* and *analog* are material references for a discernment of the world itself.

More profound and serious counter-movements could be that a growing number of people are interested in a monastic life, in places of silence and in the ascetic path of self-discovery.

Nerds in the monastery...?

Who knows? These counter-movements are unpredictable.

I find your visions still alarming, OM. You describe an increasing atrophy of the heart. When I consider the explosive development of the digital revolution, and when you say, the archetype of the nerd could become the rule, I find that extremely alarming.

It is. Another example: Finland is planning to be the first European country which no longer teaches long-hand writing in schools and instead only teaches typing on a computer. A frightening ignorance, I think. Imagine that children learn no hand writing, but learn now only to type on the keyboard. What a poor understanding of integrated human development must be the basis for this? The learning of flowing, continuous writing with a pen has not only aesthetic, artistic value, it is much more a vivid expression of the soul. I receive many letters from students. Despite some frustration with the occasional barely legible scribble, the hand written letters are my favorite. They are more honest, because they demonstrate imperfection, their humanity is more obvious. And you can also convey an emotional level, which cannot be expressed through soul-less printed letters.

Plus typing is gradually replaced by voice commands. Voice commands are taking over. "Lights on!"

The digital revolution is not limited to the virtual world, but also is going to network the physical world, as the "Internet of Things." The visionaries of the digital revolution work on the concept of the so-called "Smart Cities." This includes not only a more comprehensive video surveillance of public, urban life but also data collecting lanterns, seeing bollards, sensor laced walkways, trash cans registering explosives, everything with a direct wire to the police. In a data-gathering environment the complete monitoring is the ideal of a totally manageable, controlled, safe and secure world, every problem and every threat being solved before it even occurred. This ingenious concept is called *solutionism*, i.e., the promise to solve a problem before it appears. Before a car accident, the seeing curb, equipped with sensors of any kind sees the problem coming, has already sounded the alarm and networked other intelligent co-entities like hearing street lamps and sentient pathways, whose common data are evaluated at a central location. Orwell was yesterday.

This scenario is still utopian, but its implementation is ongoing. But on what kind of soil will this vision fall? As people's internal insecurity spreads, they become less inclined to monitor and criticize these surveillance measures. After all, these measures are finally serving the safety and security of the citizens and not the state's hunger for control. The idea of security is the mental glue holding these fantastic but not any longer distant worlds together. It is the inner anchor for an ever increasingly complex world of accelerated change. In reality, the ephemeral world was never safe, but perhaps our mind temporarily fell for the illusion of safety and security because the change in the realm of the familiar occurred at a lower frequency.

Does this mean that the mental motor for all this networked monitoring, the idea of security, is ultimately an illusion?

The idea of security comes from fear. Fear is the actual motor. Fear not felt. Fear rationalized …

Are you saying that people are caught in their inability to feel their fear?

… and in the illusion that the technical networking of the outside world can help to minimize fear and lull us into a (false) sense of security. The wisdom teachings tell us that the security of the I and its survival is fundamentally an illusion. However, there is still something else, namely the denial that the remedy is worse than the disease. As early as 2009, the German Ministry of the Interior described a "vulnerability paradox": with the number of nodes and contact points the potential vulnerabilities are increased. Ultimately a simple power failure could leave an entire metropolitan area entirely unprotected.[14] Terrorist hackers, enemy secret services, perhaps just a couple of misguided nerds trying to play a prank, in which they mess with the data networks, all this is part of the vulnerability paradox. The NSA has taught us since 9/11 that a supposedly democratic society and totalitarian, abusive surveillance measures are not necessarily mutually exclusive.

An example for this vulnerability of security systems: The terrorist organization ISIS has performed a cyber-attack on German government servers, using simulated business transactions to fraudulently receive a reimbursement over millions of Euros, which they used to buy weapons.

We are creating security, but we are losing parts of our civil liberties. Ultimately, even basic democratic rights are being limited. The limitation of our rights is legitimized by additional security. Motion patterns of people are now monitored to determine whether a person is a potential perpetrator. Ten years ago, there was a science fiction movie, in which a potential murderer was detected before he had committed the act. Simply from his purchase behavior, his motion patterns. All of this is happening now.

This is *solutionism. Solutionism* is the perfection of the illusion of security.

In the 1970s there was a large census in Germany, and there was a widespread resistance in the population, and I was very involved in it. From the present perspective, this seems pathetically harmless. At the time nobody could only begin to imagine the inexhaustible possibilities of data collection that are imminent today.

The leaders of major corporations in California, which heavily promote the digital revolution, describe its possibilities almost euphorically. Here is a quote from the book "The New Digital Age" of the former CEO of Google© Eric Schmidt:

21

"... With the help of the technology we will in the future be able to customize our devices and the entire technology in our environment exactly to our needs in order to control our whole environment according to our wishes." The whole book is filled with these utopian visions that sound like a paradise that is upon us. Everything we have just brought up is not even discussed.

These people see themselves not simply as entrepreneurs, but as visionaries with a quasi-religious mission. Larry Page of Google©, Marc Zuckerberg of Facebook©, Jeff Bezos from Amazon©, etc., want people to believe that the Garden of Eden, the vision of a better world lies in the future of an increasing mechanization and digital information networking of the outside world. The super-expansive force of these undertakings, their power of innovation, their ability to effortlessly break all limitations, not to forget the abundance of money, all this gives rise to boundless euphoria, an atmosphere of departure into a world with limitless, unprecedented possibilities: freedom itself. "Rules are made to cement existing structures. We are trying to bypass them," said the founder of the research laboratories of Google©, Sebastian Thrun.[15]

If we take the example of the private ridesharing company Uber©: In just five years, this company has expanded to over fifty countries and allegedly already has a value of around 41 billion dollars (2015); this is comparable with the value of large global corporations, which have been on the market for decades. Madness, right?

Since at least 4000 years people have traded goods across regions, but such a step change in the speed of expansion is unprecedented. The question arises: Where are the balancing, reductive mental forces of the *involutive arc,* of which we previously talked? Where are the externally limiting and inwardly directed forces that are necessary in order to allow an *integral evolution?* Where is the potential of a healthy and harmonious development in its natural frequency? In the world of wishful thinking from the book *The New Digital Age* from which you have quoted, these seem undesirable and not worth mentioning. This leads us to the crux of the matter of the real spirit, or rather thinking mind, of the digital revolution: It is the shadow of megalomania. The project behind the plans of world domination, of rapid changes in the external world (which are always secondary from an inner perspective) is the project "immortality of the ego." In an interview, the science-fiction author William Gibson talks about Peter Thiel, an Internet billionaire, co-founder of Paypal©, and one of the leading ideological heads of the digital revolution: "There are some people in the Silicon Valley, who believe in a point in history, at which humans will gain immortality because of technological progress. They expect that this will occur approximately 2040. ... Peter Thiel strives for eternal life. He is interested in a magical procedure in which the blood stream of an old person is connected to the blood stream of a young person. The old one will become younger, the young one older. The balance of interest is accomplished through a transfer payment from the old to the young."[16] Or Sebastian Thrun: "Who says that we cannot live a thousand years?"[17]. In the "World of Atoms," as

Peter Thiel calls it, the I cannot help being confronted with the miserable decay of its limited existence, but in the mental world the call for infinity is resounding. It seems to be the same call, which—incomparably more silent—came from inner masters through the generations, but was heard only by few. Is there in fact the potential of an enlightenment with technical means, or are we looking at a consistent, pathological extension of the "European dissociation," which is dominating the collective mind of the occident since 2500 years?

The true vision of the future is therefore: Obtaining immortality of the ego?

This is also a level confusion. They believe they pursue the project "immortality of the body." However, this only appears to be the same vision as that of the inner path. In reality, the vision of the inner path of awakening is exactly the opposite: The mortality of the ego. And this vision is not a vision of the future, but a vision of the *Now*.

True visionaries are only found among the scholars and masters of the inner teachings, and at the core of their teaching was neither a vision of the past nor a vision of the future, but merely a vision of *Self*-realization. From this boundless state of *Self*-fulfillment, something in the outer world develops that reflects the interior and not vice versa. From this perspective the actual development of humanity is not really relevant any more. It is left to *itSelf*. *It* knows how It develops.

When I describe the mental drive behind this extremely accelerated external development of the world, I just want to say that we cannot predict what happens when these driving factors disappear: Indolence, fear, megalomania, immortality fantasies, etc. What I predict in any case, is that any form of external hyperactivity will be reduced to a healthy level. And this *reduction* is what we urgently need to collectively heal— not endless *growth*. But who wants to hear that?

In the textbook "Intelligence of Awakening" you established a connection between the involutive arc and the way of the female soul. Does that mean that the digital revolution and its leading heads have not integrated the female soul?

With very few exceptions, the leaders are men. The digital revolution is led almost exclusively by men. The nerd is usually a male figure. We talked about the "European dissociation," which can be understood as a collective mental disorder of the occident. A mental disorder, which we have to refer to as normal. In the book *Intelligence of Awakening* I approach the same topic from a different angle. It is about at least 2000 years of continued imprisonment of the female soul. Through the basic mind-body dissociation, the I has lost the unity with the body. I (the thinking mind) *am* no longer the body, but I *have* a body. The *involutive arc* as that part of the entire *evolutive-involutive* circuit, also called the *way of the female soul*, leads back into the limitation, into the body, into matter, into the coarse physicality, into the densification of energy. Into blackness. It thus leads to the place which is also called "death." An ordinary human being is becoming a victim of the *unconscious involutive arc.* A meditator, a person of the inner practice, can and must descend the *conscious involutive arc.* For a person on the path, the way not only leads *into*, but also *through.*

The captivity of the female soul is synonymous with what L.L. Whyte in his book *The Next Development in Man* calls the "European dissociation," or it even goes beyond. This captivity is breaking the entire *involutive arc.* Not only the body is separated, but the entire path of the female soul is interrupted. It is essential to recall what such a division in an organism is causing: It is not only about an interruption, a loss, but the two disconnected entities (in this case the mind and body) form pathological disorders. L.L. Whyte: "If an organic system is split up in a specific way, the same form of distortion shows in both dissociated components. In this case, the rhythm of a holistic process becomes a double obsession. ... The constant tension and non-fulfilment bear the hallmark of the European dissociation."[18]

We have identified megalomania and the failure to respect the natural limits as a collective-mental shadow characteristic of the digital revolution and its leading ideologists. It is a classical pathological consequence of the mind-body dissociation. A mental disorder, which L.L. Whyte calls in the above quote an "obsession." The digital revolution is an obsessive act of the *evolutionary arc,* the path of the male soul, whose connection to the female soul is not available or at least incomplete.

You describe these leaders not as true visionaries because they have not understood the inner path. It is obvious that they lack wisdom, but perhaps we should ask whether this is, humanly speaking, even an adult view. The quote from the book "The New Digital Age" has something of a magical world view— shaping our environment according to our wishes. It resembles how children would view the world. Everything should obey me, I should have everything available—a flick of my finger and the moon rotates around the sun, if I want to.

Many people involved in the digital revolution show strong evidence of magical thinking and an infantile personality. Also in the structure and content of social media we find very many indications of infantile personality: Facebook is a good example. It profits from the gigantic networking, which is possible thanks to the digital revolution, so that companies and corporations will want to participate, but it is primarily a medium for adolescent, needy spirits who are looking to make a lot of "friends" to find appreciation and in order to feel important. Or think of the thousands of stupid cat and dog videos on YouTube. Are the main consumers really small children?

Upon first sight, the idea of not wanting to grow up might look like the positive intent to preserve childlike creativity and carefree attitude. These are indeed elements that are visible in the mind of Silicon Valley. (These qualities in the German collective mind—not wanting to remain a child, but having skipped childhood altogether—are rather underexposed.) However, the understanding of an adult human being of the *integral way* is different. In a healthy adult human, the child is integrated, so its qualities are not lost. A truly adult human is also childlike, and that is a good thing.

When we consider the maturing of the movement of the digital revolution, it is interesting to look at its roots. Considerable parts of it came from the anarchist and antiauthoritarian rebellious hippie movement of the 60s. Their libertarian ideas, their love of freedom, their rebellion against their parents, especially the fathers, and their refusal to take on responsibility as adults, all these elements blend into the company culture and lead to a form of playful megalomania with childish elements.

The dark side of the hippie movement, in particular of the so-called "Generation 68," is their undifferentiated disrespect to any higher authority, i.e. the fundamental lack of distinction between true and false authority. In the mind of the leading heads of the digital revolution, the same indicators are evident. Governments, politicians, leaders, whole countries, they all are representative of the archetype of the father, and his troublesome boundaries as an act of authority are seen as outdated and need to be circumvented. "We do not get around," says American cultural scientist Fred Turner, "one thing: the liberating forces that we have unleashed to create a communal, post-sixties world have, in effect, created a surveillance economy and an authoritarian leader."[19] He means the election of US President Donald Trump. I might as well extend the context to the massive occurrence of collective, regressive-authoritarian tendencies in many European countries. Disintegrated love of freedom, the total unleashing of the thinking mind—in other words: megalomania—forces the return of those wrongful limitations by the hands of just that authority, which was supposed to be removed from reality in the first place. This is an irony of fate in the closed world of the thinking mind, in which the opposite of the supposedly true intention is always generated.

It is quite interesting to see how the neo-liberalism is coming from this source, i.e., from an originally good intention to unmask false authorities, but then overshoots its intention and no longer recognizes any higher authority. What follows is a limitless expansion, which respects neither political boundaries, nor borders between countries, nor limits of privacy protection. I have never seen it like this before.

Facebook© is a good example. It is hypocritical to immediately delete any figure of a naked person (even pictures of Greek statues with visible genitals are deleted), while gross, mental dirt, e.g. with delusional fascist or racist content, coarse insults, hate speech, etc. may simply remain and only is deleted upon request, and only reluctantly. If at all. This is a lack of adult responsibility.

It is not specific for the age of digitalization, but for all of the technology development in history that each technology is advertised as allowing greater convenience. How do you explain from the point of view of the wisdom teachings this attraction of convenience? Is it really a true need that everything becomes more and more convenient, so that in the

29

end you can do everything with a voice command or a snap of a finger? What is actually so attractive?

There are needs of the soul, and there are needs of the mind, which we must differentiate. Convenience is one of the main needs of the ego-mind. However, this is not just about convenience, but in particular also about speed. Greed requires speed to be able to gobble up more and more information in ever shorter time, because it is the purpose of greed to fill inner holes. Since these holes are bottomless, they must constantly be refilled.

However, the distinction between the needs of the soul and the needs of the thinking mind cannot be taught through technology. Any form of technology per se is neither good nor bad, but merely a set of tools, an extended arm, but for whom? That is the question. In whose service? The Internet is a great source of information. Wikipedia© for example, which was initially ridiculed, has an unprecedented success story, and I appreciate it very much. It contains a large part of general knowledge that the brain does not have to store any more. And it is accessible from anywhere. This also changes the old view on the acquisition of school knowledge by mindless repetition. Not all factual knowledge needs to be stored in the brain, I can retrieve it with just a few mouse clicks from the Internet. This empties the mind of non-essential detailed knowledge about the world, about what is known. A large part of this accumulated second hand knowledge is nothing other than substitute knowledge. Substitute for true knowledge, which is not present, but which is very much needed: The knowledge of *Reality.* Of the unknown. A knowledge, which can only be obtained first hand, through direct and lived experience.

So it is all a question of who uses the tools?

The tech-visionaries are praising the tools and their possibilities. As if they themselves were the ultimate source of happiness. Another level confusion. It needs a teaching, which can transmit such a distinction in the first place. It needs to be a teaching, which does not get lost in the external tools, but which directs the attention inwards and gives access to a knowledge about the great distinction of the Inner Path: Ego and non-ego. Soul and mind. Reality and illusion. Through this attention shift the external tools are increasingly losing their importance. They rapidly sink on the scale of inner values. An object such as a smartphone is good, but has it an existential value? No. Do I really need it? No. Apple©? Never heard of it. Once again to directly answer your question: The lure is in the fulfillment of substitute needs. At the expense of the real needs of the soul.

This means that in order for this increasing influence of technologies not to turn into a nightmare for the individual we need distinctive teachings, inner teachings, which contain the knowledge of the Self and the non-Self. And then you have talked about the fact that it also involves feeling what you actually don't want to feel so that the inner emotional factors get recognized, e.g. fear.

Let us imagine the following utopia: Imagine, fear as drive for outer expansive mechanization suddenly falls away. Nobody has fear any more. The drive to the external has disappeared from one second to the next, and the attention naturally falls back inward. Sometimes people just sit there and are completely aware of their *Being*, because the need of a hyperactive doer, whose primary drive is the compensation of subconscious fear, has simply disappeared...

... that starts already with speaking ...

… yes, it starts with speaking, and the digitization opens almost limitless possibilities for verbal expression in written or spoken form. It is therefore potentially an excellent catalyst for the ego at the rational level of awareness, an ego-distributor. A large part of the rational human communication is not about content— you could use a fraction of the words to possibly communicate much clearer—it is exclusively about the compensation of unconscious fear. Fear is the hidden cause of many unnecessary words. Without fear, we only need a fraction of the talk. A much larger part would be communicated in silence. Without words. *Does this mean that there is also a collective increase of fear? Earlier, in the Middle Ages, one could say that people even should have had much more need to be fearful, because it really was about life and death?*

This is indeed the question, whether the people in the Middle Ages really had more fear. The more security we create in the outer life, the more the supposed ability to plan and control the supposed death increases, the more fear we have. The aforementioned megalomania, the project "immortality of the ego" by mentalization in the digital revolution, is nothing other than a *rationalization of* unconscious, of inaccessible fear. The further we remove ourselves from direct encounter with death and impermanence the more we cut ourselves off from the *involutive arc*, and the greater will be the fear in our subconscious. Rationally, this is a paradox, and I am quite sure that for someone like Peter Thiel (most likely an Enneatype 6, fear-fixated) this connection is not present, because it means that he actually achieves the opposite of what he really intends to. He wants inviolability through immortality, while his unconscious level of fear increases constantly.

We can say that this megalomania also has a true core in some respect? I get the feeling that the human being strives to be equal to God. He wants to create a machine that is smarter, hears better, sees better, and is immortal. A new crown of creation.

There is a true core in everything. The human pioneer spirit is unstoppable, and the increasingly complex technologies of digitization are also the expression of this natural pioneer spirit, that creates the unstoppably growing complexity which is nothing else but an expression of increasingly differentiated intelligence. In the *integral Evolution* this is a complexity founded in total simplicity, and both are not excluding each other. However, the *internal/external level confusion* has led to a dramatically overemphasized importance of the outer worlds, a failure through ignorance.

This means that the robots will come?

The robots, the bodies of digitization, will come, and they will take over more and more areas of life including human privacy. It is only a matter of time until there are humanoid robots. At the University of Osaka, an engineer has developed a clone of himself, with a silicone skin, which is hardly distinguishable from himself. "The very young and the very old cannot distinguish between man and clone very well," he says, "We have therefore conducted experiments in nursing homes with robots as nurses or entertainers, and the results were really positive."[20] In Japan, robots are embraced enthusiastically. There is even a hotel entirely run by robots. In school education robots are already used, as well as in nursing care for the elderly. Most Europeans are not as receptive, they focus more on the dark side: the glorification of the machine over the human condition.

The old story of the sorcerer's apprentice comes to mind: "Spirits that I've cited, my commands ignore."

At Oxford University there is an institute called the "Future of Humanity Institute." They deal exclusively with scenarios of runaway machines, which could turn against humans. The director of this institute, Nick Bostrom, has written a book: *Superintelligence: Paths, Dangers, Strategies.* How could such a superintelligence arise? "A self-learning, self-improving system could eventually start to strive for more—more computing capacity, more memory and more information, more control over other computers, networks and devices. This machine intelligence would become autonomous, secretly seek domination of external data centers ... before it would get ready for the final blow: against competing automated systems and against the people that stand in the way of their quest."[21] Of course, this scenario still is science fiction, but many of these fantasies become real, because the thinking mind pursues the realization of exactly these fantasies vigorously. The struggle of the people against runaway machines is a major subject in science fiction. This fight will come. Nobody can predict, in what form and to what extent, but it will come.

An inner teaching, a wisdom teaching, which is able to translate the universal laws of the cosmos, views external operations as "signatures," imprints of the mind. So if we look at this issue from the internal point of view: Machines assume power over the whole of humanity. Let us remember that Gurdjieff used this term of the machine, it was a central concept of his teaching. People are machines, he said. And the inner teachings are concerned precisely with this question: How can a human being become human?

This was long before the digital revolution.

Precisely. Machines taking over people—from the point of view of an inner teaching, this has long been done. The machine is another name for the thinking mind. No need to fear machines, firstly because the takeover has already happened, and secondly because the machine itself is no embodiment of evil. Evil is the soulless, gaining its own momentum, turning against the living. It is specifically *the machine assuming its own life*, which is a symbol of the evil. This is what we should fear, internally as well as externally. Because it represents the assumption of the living—until it appears to be alive itself. Therefore the wisdom teachings emphasize the distinction between illusion—the dead appearing to be alive—and reality—life across a series of octaves. Love and truth, every form of authentic spirituality is always based on what is alive.

A robot will never be able to give rise to divine consciousness. Superintelligence—referring to the title of the book—is a misguided, a misleading term. It is based on a partial, a disintegrated understanding of intelligence. A robot will never obtain *integral intelligence* as the wisdom teachings understand and know it. Of course scientists try to teach robots to feel or, more specifically, to perfectly mimic an expression of feelings. This is a world of difference. Perhaps for small children and for senile people it may be the same whether you encounter a humanoid or meet a human being. But even if it is not perceived consciously, it still makes a difference, because the Chi[22] will not be the same. Where there is no Chi, no life is to be found—and thus no soul.

Feelings of highly developed people in any case cannot be seen with outer eyes but only with inner eyes. Let us not forget:

Even a learning robot is only as developed as the mental horizon of its programmer. This means that its learning will remain purely horizontal in nature. It will never be able to accomplish a vertical ascent to a higher level of consciousness. Because such an ascent requires a transcendent process in the consciousness, and those who believe that it could be taught to a machine have fundamentally misunderstood the nature of consciousness.

A beautiful image: Robots have no inner eyes.
I would like to conclude with a question about Gut Saunstorf, Place of Stillness. You are the founder of the monastery Gut Saunstorf—are places like these also a way of healing for this exact scenario, which we discussed today? The monastic community, or the spirit of a monastery?

Monastic life is based on renunciation, the ascetic path. Since the middle ages came to an end and the age of enlightenment began to take hold—a process that lasted several hundred years—this path has been increasingly ignored in a profane society. In order to gain knowledge of the *Self*, the willingness to renounce the world is necessary. When the path of the abandonment of the world, which is leading outside the world, opens the access to *reality*, is allowing the realization of the *Self*, a new kind of contemplative awareness of the world can emerge. Then the human being is in the world but not of the world.

The text is based on interviews of students with OM C. Parkin.

End Notes

1 **OM C. Parkin**, *Intelligence of Awakening: Navigating the Wisdom Path*, Gateways Books and Tapes, available April 2019.

2 *Reality* refers to the reality of the limitless spirit, in which we rest, when the self-created world of the limited thinking mind is recognized as an illusion and is transcended. *Reality* refers to the eternal truth, beyond all transient phenomena and is free of any conditions.

3 **Jean Gebser** (1905 - 1973), Swiss-German cultural philosopher and consciousness researcher. Main work (quoted here): *The Ever-Present Origin* deals with the developmental stages: the archaic, magical, mythical, and mental stages towards the Integral Consciousness. These developmental steps are carried out by mutation (transformation), whereby the higher levels contain the preceding levels. He assumes that the presently prevailing mental consciousness is mutating collectively into the Integral Consciousness.

4 In the author's vocabulary, which often invokes the original word etymologies, the German term "Geistigung" (spiritualization) describes an integral ascent of human consciousness from gross to subtle matter, whereas the term "Ver-Geistigung" (mentalization) describes a non-integral ascent into a mental world, such as happens with many philosophers, theologians and scholars.

5 **OM C. Parkin**, Integrales Yoga, in: *Gelebte Spiritualität – Wege der Annäherung*, Reihe *advaita*, Bd. 3, S.15-23; advaitaMedia 2012

6 **Involutive arc**: Part of the eternal process of becoming, which can energetically only be understood in conjunction with the evolutionary arc. Details of this can be found in *Intelligence of Awakening*, see Note 1.

7 **The fourth brain:** The boundless, intelligence "center," outside of space and time, removed from the dualist perceptions of the thinking mind, which transcends the three brains (intelligence/awareness centers: physical, emotional, mental).

8 **tamas-like**: *Tamas* is in Indian philosophy the lowest and most uncouth of the three *gunas,* those basic properties of the structures of all the objects in the physical world. In the human spirit *tamas* presents itself as inertia, dullness, ignorance and absence of discernment. *Tamas forgetfulness* describes the common form of forgetting as a subconscious act of mental loss.

9 See Ken Wilber, *Up From Eden: A Transpersonal View of Human Evolution*

10 **The Enneagram:** An esoteric cosmology that describes the basic laws of the cosmos: *The Law of Three* (in Christianity the Holy Trinity) as the basic principle of the cosmos, and *the Law of Seven* as the principle of creation, in which this trinity unfolds and communicates. These two laws form the symbol of the *Enneagram.* The *Enneagram* 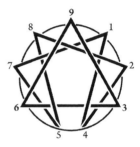 of Character Fixations* is applied to symbolize structures and loss of reality of the human mind. *Subjective Enneagrams* (like the *Enneagram of Passions*, or the *Enneagram of Defense Structures*) describe reality losses of personal worlds, while the *Objective Enneagrams* describe reality as it *is*. Part of the *Objective Enneagrams* is the *Enneagram of Holy Ideas.*

11 **Fixations**: Usually unconscious crystallizations of thought patterns in the spiritual development of the child, which constitute the adult I, lacking self-reflection. A fixation can have its focus in the first (physical), second (emotional) or third (mental) brain. The *Enneagram of Character Fixations* (see note 9) symbolizes nine lawfully resulting character structures.

12 **Rationalization:** A defense mechanism of the ego mind against unpleasant or threatening impulses from the first (physical) and second (emotional) brain, being replaced through mental ("reasonable") constructs. The original perception is sinking into the subconscious.

13 DIE ZEIT, 5/12/2016, "All you can read"

14 DIE ZEIT, 11/26/2015, "Sie sieht, sie hört, sie lebt"

15 DER SPIEGEL 2/28/2015, „Das Morgen-Land"

16 ZEITMAGAZIN Nr.3/2017

17 DER SPIEGEL 2/28/2015, „Das Morgen-Land"

18 See Ken Wilber, *Up From Eden: A Transpersonal View of Human Evolution*, 1981

19 DIE ZEIT 3/23/2017, "Die Hippies sind Schuld"; p.32

20 DIE ZEIT 12/17/2014, "Sein unheimlicher Klon"; p.32

21 DIE ZEIT 5/12/2016, "Dieser Mann denkt über den Untergang der Menschheit nach," p. 29

22 **Chi** / also *Qi*: In the view of the culture of Ancient China and of Daoism, *Chi* permeates everything that exists and happens. As a cosmic energy principle *Chi* is neither physical nor mental in nature. *Chi* remains unaffected by any change.

###

42

OM C. Parkin

Mystic, Philosopher and Author.
Director of a Contemporary Inner School in Germany.

OM studied psychology, but dropped out of university studies after 3 years, because it gave him no real insight into human nature. In parallel, he worked intensely on the spiritual tradition of Sufism and the Enneagram as a mirror of the cosmos, especially the human psyche. In 1990, at the age of 27, he suffered a serious car accident, crossed the threshold of death, and woke up again to life, egolessly. Shortly thereafter, he met his spiritual teacher Gangaji, who helped him process his transformation, which cut through the everyday world of experience. Gangaji sent OM to her own teacher H. W. L. Poonja, a direct disciple of Ramana Maharshi, who gave OM his spiritual name.

OM C. Parkin has been teaching orally and in writing ever since, accompanying people in their search for truth and self-knowledge at spiritual events (Darshan). In addition, OM C. Parkin is the author of a variety of books, writings and articles. He founded the first major German-speaking mystery school of the present time in the 90s.

Since 2010, the school is located at Gut Saunstorf, a splendidly restored historic manor house near the Hanseatic city of Wismar, that has been known as the "Ort der Stille" (Place of

Stillness). As a modern monastery, it is also open as a retreat for people who are on the inner path.

OM C. Parkin's spiritual teaching, also referred to as Inner Science, is based on the Eastern Advaita tradition (teaching of non-duality. The best known representative of this tradition in the West is Ramana Maharshi). This teaching also encompasses Western experiential paths (e. g. Christian Mysticism, Georges I. Gurdjieff: The Fourth Way) as well as modern psychological and psychotherapeutic methods. The goal is self-knowledge through inner work, which ultimately leads to the realization of the true human nature.

Contact: www.om-c-parkin.com

Intelligence of Awakening: Navigating the Wisdom Path

430 pages, $29.95 trade paperback
ISBN: 978-0-89556-284-5
Available in April, 2019, from Gateways Books and Tapes

This book illuminates the path to liberation for those who turn inward, beyond the boundaries of religious denominations, and rise above the attachments in life in order to attain knowledge of their true nature.

Gut Saunstorf—Place of Stillness
A Modern Monastery.

Do you need a specific place to experience stillness? Where can I meet OM C. Parkin and find out about Perennial Philosophy?

An Inviting Place

Since 2010, Gut Saunstorf near Wismar at the Baltic Sea, has served as a monastic place of stillness, led by the spiritual teacher OM C. Parkin. The desire and goal was to lend a place to OM's teaching and work and to give a home to a growing community. In Gut Saunstorf, the ruins of a manor house, which was in danger of collapsing, have been transformed into a graceful and silent place that is open to the members of the Sangha as well as the general public. Gut Saunstorf extends an invitation to all who seek rest and want to engage with their true Self in inner retreat. A sacred place: Elegant in its appearance, Gut Saunstorf lends itself in a unique way to retreats into the deep inner Self.

A Modern Monastery

Gut Saunstorf realizes the vision of an interdenominational

spiritual center in which both Western and Eastern spiritual teachings and therapies are taught and practiced. The *Enneallionce - School of Inner Work* is located here, and has hosted many events, conferences and ongoing groups. On a regular basis, seekers have the opportunity to meet OM C. Parkin in *Darshan*, whether as active students or as visitors, who are seeking stillness and inner retreat.

Place of Stillness

Gut Saunstorf as a place of retreat and contemplation is dedicated to the rediscovery of inner peace and stillness. The building and its serene surroundings create a monastic atmosphere, conducive to inner transformation, in a sacred place. Whoever enters will experience something new. Take off your shoes, become quiet, enter into a state of mindfulness for people and things. Experience delicious vegetarian meals in silence. Enjoy the artifacts from various religious traditions at the core of the Perennial Philosophy.

Contact: www.kloster-saunstorf.de